CW00949702

CALISTHENIC⌐ ⌐⌐⌐

SENIORS

The 8-Week Calisthenics Workouts For Seniors To Improve Balance And Build Strength

JENNY MACKLIN

ISBN: 9798378528325

Table of Contents

The Correct and Incorrect Types of Pain

A Heartbeat

Dizziness

Breathe Control Issues

THE SENIOR CALISTHENICS PROGRAM

Weeks 1 & 2

Weeks 3 & 4

(Monday — Strength)

[Wednesday — Endurance]

Friday — Flexibility/Balance]

Weeks 5 & 6

[Monday — Strength]

Wednesday — Endurance]

Friday — Flexibility/Balance]

WEEKS 7 & 8

[Monday — Strength]

Wednesday — Endurance]

[Friday — Flexibility/Balance]

INTRODUCTION

The 8-Week Calisthenics for Seniors Program is pleased to have you.

If you're not acquainted with us, we're A Shot of Adrenaline, an online community for fitness enthusiasts committed to assisting individuals in achieving their fitness objectives and living their best lives via calisthenics, sometimes known as "bodyweight training."

The information that follows is a thorough, simple-to-follow program created especially for elderly adults wanting to lay a foundation for physical health, using the advice and analysis of specialists in the area of senior fitness.

We do need to make a small disclaimer before continuing:

While being well studied, this free tool is not a "catch-all" answer for all problems. Before making any dietary changes or starting a new fitness regimen, seniors, particularly those suffering from conditions like joint discomfort, arthritis, recent injuries, or any other physical limitations, should always speak with their doctor. Although it's necessary to push yourself, it's even more crucial to pay attention to your body and avoid pushing it over its breaking point.

WHY HAVE A SENIOR PROGRAM?

We are really fortunate to have a large and varied group of fitness fans. We work with individuals who have spent their whole life actively interested in fitness as well as others who have never worked out a day in their lives. No matter where you are in your fitness journey, we aim to provide something for everyone so that we can be a resource for you.

Senior individuals make up a large component of our online community (people over the age of

65). While we offer other low-impact programs for beginning, such the Calisthenics for Beginners program, we recognized that nothing we had was a good place for elders to start and that they too should feel included.

Also, there aren't many online programs created especially for elders. A person could get discouraged as a result and lose interest in trying to become in shape. This is something that we vehemently oppose. We don't want seniors to believe they don't need to exercise, which is even more vital. Everyone, even elders, should be physically active.

The National Institute on Aging suggests engaging in endurance exercise for 30 minutes most days of the week:

On most or all days of the week, try to work up to at least 30 minutes of exercise that causes you to breathe heavily. Each day is ideal. Since it increases your energy or "staying power," that exercise is referred to be an endurance one. It's not necessary to work out for 30 minutes straight. It's okay to take ten minutes at once.

Being elderly is not a cause to slow down, according to the National Institute of Health's Senior Health program:

Everyone, benefits, even older adults from regular physical activity and exercise for both their physical and mental health. Regular exercise and being physically active may enhance long-term health and even help some elderly adults who already have illnesses and impairments.

So, according to health professionals, older individuals should strive to remain as active as possible.

Also, being physically active allows you to fully appreciate your senior years. It is being able to engage in activities that make you genuinely autonomous, such as playing catch with your grandkids, dancing at a family wedding, enjoying gardening, etc.

A Shot of Adrenaline's little team is fortunate to have many seniors in our life, including parents, grandparents, aunts and uncles, friends, colleagues, etc. Despite the fact that none of us are seniors, we are convinced that you are, too. And we want for everyone to be able to fully fulfill their life. You don't have to quit being active just because you've reached your "golden years," right?

We only got one body, after all. And for as long as we own it, it is our duty to take care of it. By doing this, you will be able to improve both your own life and the lives of people around you. At A Shot of Adrenaline, that is essentially what we are all about. For us, it's not about working out for many hours each day to get a shredded body with protruding muscles. As corny as it may seem, we want you to be able to experience life to the fullest, and having a body that can function to its maximum potential is essential to that.

TYPICAL SENIOR CONCERNS

Having said that, some seniors may still have valid worries when contemplating a new workout regimen. Now let's spend a little time addressing as many of them as we can.

I'm too old To Work Out.

Not at all, no! We've spoken about this before, but exercise is just as vital for seniors as it is for everyone else. You don't have to start accepting certain restrictions just because you become older. In fact, a sedentary lifestyle may be more to blame for many of those limits than anything else. Johns Hopkins University School of Medicine's assistant professor of geriatrics and gerontology, Alicia I. Arbaje, MD, MPH, states Many of the signs of aging that we connect with becoming older, such weakness and balance issues, are really signs of inactivity rather than getting older.

I Have Not Worked Out In A Very Long Time (Or Ever).

I understand. You don't have to jump right back in. That is to say, even if you shouldn't plan to run a marathon any time soon, you may still make tiny, gradual progress toward a solid workout program.

You should start with the calisthenics program that lasts for eight weeks. We start with the fundamentals and work our way up in a framework that is meant to help you develop. You will identify as an athlete after this eight-week trip is over!

My Generation Doesn't Exercise,

Not so certain! There are many folks in their latter years that are still going strong. even making the younger generation envious of their skills!

Please have a look at our post on amazing physical accomplishments performed by older folks from the age of 50 to the late 80s. After you see what these individuals have accomplished and what you are really capable of, we are certain that you will be inspired.

Arthritis

As the deputy director of the National Institute on Aging and a geriatrician, Marie Bernard, MD, notes, "Arthritis is perhaps the most common ailment that adults 65 or older deal with."

About half (49.7) of all individuals over 65, according to the Centers for Disease Control and Prevention, have arthritis. Many are aware of the pain and suffering it may bring about as well as how it can make it difficult to participate in beloved physical activities.

Nonetheless, it's crucial to keep moving forward despite this. The Mayo Clinic states that exercise is essential for those who have arthritis. "It helps you fight tiredness, improves strength and flexibility, and lessens joint discomfort... Even little exercise might reduce your discomfort and assist you in maintaining a healthy weight.

Recent Harm

Those who have just sustained an injury may resume their fitness routine if it is done cautiously and sensibly, just as others who haven't worked out in a long time or at all. How long does it take? It does, of course. Healing from injuries might take weeks or even months. But, if you see your doctor and slowly work your way back into basic activities like flexibility and balance, you should be able to get back into the swing of things.

And keep in mind: keep going even if it seems like you aren't making any progress. Our bodies may alter in a variety of ways, some of which are more obvious than others.

THE ADVANTAGES OF EXERCISE AS YOU AGE

We've previously spoken about how seniors with conditions like arthritis and recent injuries might benefit from exercise, but that's not what this article is about! We want you to fully understand the advantages of exercising as a senior.

Disease Delays or Prevents

- It has been shown that exercise is a crucial element in avoiding or postponing illnesses. A physical exercise program offered a slight boost in cognition for persons with subjective memory impairment, according to one research. According to the National Parkinson Foundation, exercise is crucial to preserving balance, movement, and daily living skills for persons with Parkinson's disease (PD). According to the American Diabetes Association, more activity increases insulin's effectiveness by making your cells more responsive to it. This implies that they can also remove glucose from the circulation during exercise utilizing a process entirely different from insulin.

- It has also been shown that an exercise program may reduce osteoarthritis symptoms.

- Age raises your chance of having high blood pressure, but exercise may help keep it under control. Being more active may actually reduce your systolic blood pressure, which is the highest number in a blood pressure measurement, by an average of 4 to 9 millimeters of mercury, according to the Mayo Clinic (mm Hg). It is comparable to several blood pressure medicines.

Reduces Stress and Elevates Mood

- If you believe that fretting about working out and then actually doing it would only make your mental health worse, you're mistaken. Several studies have shown that regular exercise improves your mood. Even the possibility of using an exercise training program in place of medicines to treat depression in older people has been raised.

- Regular, moderate physical exercise may help manage stress and enhance mood, according to the National Institute of Health, Senior Health.

Enables You to Pursue Your Passions

- Consider the activities that you really appreciate. The key is that it doesn't have to be physically demanding. We think that regular exercise may benefit almost every part of your daily life, and evidence supports this idea. It implies that you are free to pursue your passions. a few instances

- Play with your grandkids while keeping up with them.
- During a family wedding, dance
- Grow your own vegetables
- During a pool party, swim
- Without regard to physical constraints
- With pals, play cards or other games.
- Read the books you like.
- Use your creative expression
- And a lot more

Greater Independent

We want to be independent beginning in our early adolescence, and sometimes much earlier. There is a yearning that never goes away, but sadly, our bodies can. Physical restrictions are the most frequent cause of a senior losing their independence. They may sometimes be avoided because of an illness or heredity. To preserve independence, though, a regular exercise routine is essential. After all, independence might help us feel more purposeful and enable us to accomplish our other objectives. Exercise may both prevent impairment and reduce the chance of an episode of disability, according to a Lifestyle Intervention and Independence for Elderly study.

WHY DO BODYWEIGHT EXERCISES?

You may be wondering why we're so committed to calisthenics, or bodyweight training, if you're contemplating trying this program.

1. The fact is that we don't want to sound like other fitness businesses who assert that their products are "the Greatest." For some people, calisthenics are a terrific alternative; for others, not so much. There are a few reasons why we like it and believe seniors will too.

No need for a large initial investment is benefit number one.

The fact that very little to no equipment is required for calisthenics training is a huge advantage.

Because there is no equipment required, you may begin training without spending a lot of money. Of course, as you develop, certain equipment (such as a pull-up bar, rings, etc.) may become required, but compared to weight training, where pricey equipment eventually becomes essential, the investment is still extremely minimal. (Other weight training techniques, such, for instance, sandbag training, also offer the same benefit.)

2. You Can Train Anywhere.

As specific equipment is not required, the first benefits direct outcome of being able to practice anywhere.

This was one among the factors that contributed to calisthenics first appealing to me as a kind of exercise.

The freedom to exercise anywhere you choose is a huge benefit that few other training methods provide. This manner, you may maintain top physical condition wherever you are and it will be extremely difficult for you to skip exercises due to circumstances (such as while traveling).

3. Target Multiple Qualities At Once

You will face challenges in a variety of ways as you develop towards advanced calisthenics movements, not only in terms of your maximum power.

You will therefore develop your strength, balance, mobility, flexibility, etc.

Moreover, calisthenics will help you develop a strong sense of body control, kinesthetic awareness, and overall body awareness.

4. Safety

As comparison to utilizing equipment or lifting big weights, calisthenics is inherently safer. Your muscles and joints will be under less stress if you weigh less. This applies to everyone, not just the elderly. We strongly think that a workout should be as simple as possible since "less is more," in other words. When you already have all the equipment you need for a workout, why feel like you need to depend on a sophisticated machine?

Those with arthritis, joint discomfort, or other common aging ailments might benefit greatly from bodyweight exercises.

THINGS TO LOOK OUT FOR WHILE WORKING OUT

When completing this program, we definitely want you to push yourself. You're really far more competent than you may realize. Of course, there are safeties measures that we want to make sure you are aware of.

The Correct and Incorrect Types of Pain

No pain, no gain is a saying that, for the most part, is accurate. While exercising, you must be willing to push yourself over your apparent boundaries. It applies to people of all ages. Yet it's crucial to know the difference between healthy discomfort and danger signs.

Having soreness and a sense of tightness in your muscles, for instance, is often a sign that your muscles are receiving blood flow and are capable of engaging in hypertrophy, which causes them to get larger and more toned.

Any soreness outside of your muscles and pain in your joints that lasts more than a few days are typically not healthy. If any of these occur, be sure you can tell the difference and get medical attention.

A Heartbeat

A really helpful graphic from the American Heart Association explains what a healthy heart rate during exercise is (as well as how to calculate it). It is recommended that a senior's average maximum heart rate fall between 150 and 155 beats per minute. If it's too high, you're straining and need to go more slowly.

Once again, it's fantastic that you're pushing yourself, but we want to make sure you're doing it under control.

Dizziness

One of those symptoms, experiencing dizziness while exercising, may be brought on by both problematic and non-painful events. It may be as easy as dehydration or over-exertion, as Health.com advises; in that case, make sure you drink plenty of water and keep in mind what we stated about not pushing yourself too hard.

But, if you have dizziness even after modest activity, it may be an indication of exercise-induced asthma. If so, your doctor could advise you to use an inhaler before working out. Dizziness, however, may also be a sign of an arrhythmia or an irregular heartbeat. If you believe you may have an arrhythmia, you should consult with your doctor. Treatments for these conditions might vary.

Breathe Control Issues

Getting out of breath when exercising is generally considered to be normal; after all, if you pushed yourself hard, you should expect to feel exhausted. Yet much like dizziness, you should see your doctor if you have shortness of breath while doing little activity or perhaps no exercise at all. Remember, there are several potential explanations for this, so if you see it often, make an appointment with your doctor.

Dehydration

While exercising, you need to make sure you're receiving enough water. It's important to be hydrated for your general health, and dehydration during exercise might have negative effects. Watch out for the early warning symptoms, such as weariness, cramps, or a rapid heartbeat, and always have a bottle close by.

Keep in mind that drinking water doesn't only need to happen before a workout; it should happen all day long.

THE SENIOR CALISTHENICS PROGRAM

Well, let's start working now!

The 8-week Calisthenics for Seniors Program is divided into 4 portions, which are Weeks 1-2, Weeks 3–4, Weeks 5–6, and Weeks 7-8, as you can see. The first portion is where we advise you to at least start; if you find it too simple, you may go on to another. But first, be sure you are doing each exercise with the proper form. Your ability to complete the tasks correctly is considerably more crucial than how quickly you go through the course.

During the first two weeks, you'll have a walking assignment in addition to the exercises you'll see in this section.

Walking provides several health advantages for all of us, particularly for seniors, including a lower chance of heart disease, improved balance, weight reduction, and a host of other advantages.

Please don't skip out on your walking assignments; they're just as crucial as the workouts. Try to finish this walking assignment every week, not just the first two, if you can.

The prescribed walking time is 60–120 minutes each week. This may be divided into multiple days; in fact, we advise it. To reach your desired time, try to walk for 10 to 20 minutes each day.

WEEKS 1 & 2

WEEK 1 - 2

Neck stretch
3 sets of 10 seconds

Shoulder rolls
10 forward/10 backward

Arm circles (big)
10 forward/10 backward

Arm circles (big)
10 forward/10 backward

Towel stretch
30 seconds/arm

Calf stretch
5/leg for 10 seconds

Quad stretch
5 sets of 3 seconds/leg

Knee hugs in chair
5 sets of 5 seconds/leg

Bodyweight half squats
3 sets of 5

Hip bridge on ground
3 sets of 3 seconds each

Trunk twists
5/side for 2 seconds

+

Walking assignment: walk 60-120 minutes per week. This can be broken up
into different days -- in fact, we recommend it that way. Try walking
10-20 minutesa day to get to your goal time.

WEEKS 3 & 4

(Monday — Strength)

WEEK 3 - 4

MONDAY

Wall Pushes
3 sets of 6

Leg kick in chair
3 sets of 6/leg

Bodyweight squats with chair
3 sets of 5

Self arm wrestling
3 sets of 20 seconds/arm

Palm pushes
3 sets of 20 seconds

Field goal pushes
3 sets of 20 seconds

Calf raises w/ chair
3 sets of 20 seconds

High wall sits
3 sets of 15 seconds

[Wednesday — Endurance]

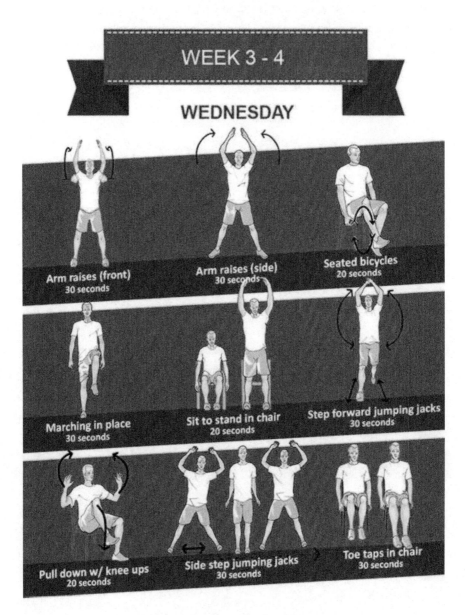

WEEK 3 - 4

WEDNESDAY

Arm raises (front)
30 seconds

Arm raises (side)
30 seconds

Seated bicycles
20 seconds

Marching in place
30 seconds

Sit to stand in chair
20 seconds

Step forward jumping jacks
30 seconds

Pull down w/ knee ups
20 seconds

Side step jumping jacks
30 seconds

Toe taps in chair
30 seconds

Repeat 2 times for 3 total sets

Friday — Flexibility/Balance]

WEEK 3 - 4

FRIDAY

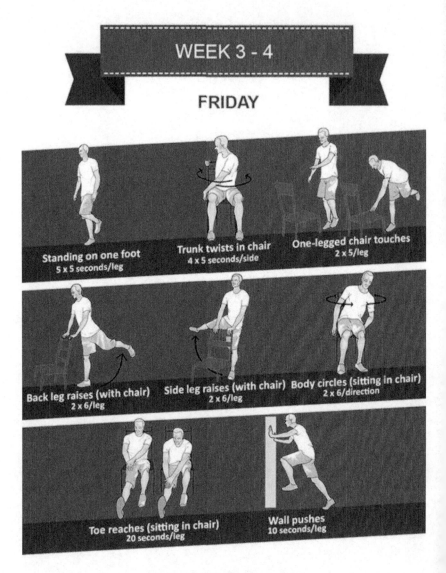

Standing on one foot
5 x 5 seconds/leg

Trunk twists in chair
4 x 5 seconds/side

One-legged chair touches
2 x 5/leg

Back leg raises (with chair)
2 x 6/leg

Side leg raises (with chair)
2 x 6/leg

Body circles (sitting in chair)
2 x 6/direction

Toe reaches (sitting in chair)
20 seconds/leg

Wall pushes
10 seconds/leg

Repeat 1 time for 2 total sets

WEEKS 5 & 6

[Monday — Strength]

WEEK 5 - 6

MONDAY

Push ups on knees
3 sets of 5

Self arm wrestling
3 sets of 30 seconds/arm

Palm pushes
3 sets of 30 seconds

Field goal pushes
3 sets of 3 seconds

Calf raises (no chair)
3 sets of 20 seconds

Leg kick w/ 1 second hold
3 sets of 5/leg

Bodyweight squats w/ chair
3 sets of 7

High wall sits
3 sets of 20 seconds

Push ups on knees — 3 sets of 5

Wednesday — Endurance]

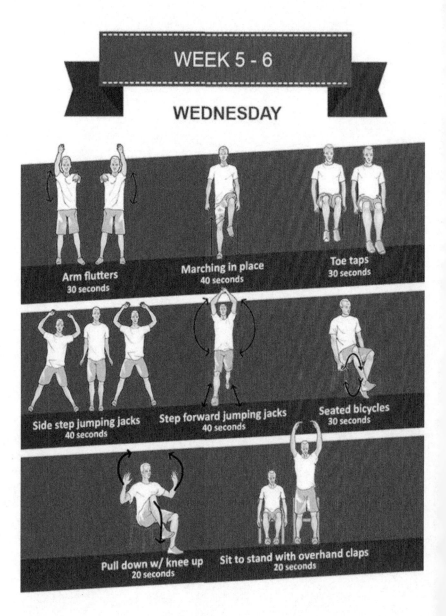

WEEK 5 - 6

WEDNESDAY

Arm flutters
30 seconds

Marching in place
40 seconds

Toe taps
30 seconds

Side step jumping jacks
40 seconds

Step forward jumping jacks
40 seconds

Seated bicycles
30 seconds

Pull down w/ knee up
20 seconds

Sit to stand with overhand claps
20 seconds

Friday — Flexibility/Balance]

WEEK 5 - 6

FRIDAY

Standing on one foot
8 seconds/leg

Trunk twists in chair
4 x 5 seconds/side

One-legged chair touches
7/leg

Back leg raises (with chair)
8/leg

Side leg raises (with chair)
8/leg

Body circles (sitting in chair)
8/direction

Toe reaches (sitting in chair)
30 seconds/leg

Wall pushes
15 seconds/leg

Repeat 1 time for 2 total sets

WEEKS 7 & 8

[Monday — Strength]

WEEK 7 - 8

MONDAY

Push ups
3 sets of 5

Self arm wrestling
3 sets of 40 seconds/arm

Palm pushes
3 sets of 40 seconds

Field goal pushes
3 sets of 40 seconds

Calf raises (no chair)
3 sets of 20 seconds

Leg kick w/ 1 second hold
3 sets of 7/leg

Bodyweight squats
3 sets of 5

High wall sits
3 sets of 30 seconds

Push ups — 3 sets of 5

Wednesday — Endurance]

WEEK 7 - 8

WEDNESDAY

Arm flutters
40 seconds

High knees
20 seconds

Toe taps
30 seconds

Jumping jacks
30 seconds

Stair step ups
30 seconds

Seated bicycles
20 seconds

Pull down w/ knee up
20 seconds

Sit to stand with overhand claps
30 seconds

Repeat 2 times for 3 total sets

[Friday — Flexibility/Balance]

WEEK 7 - 8

FRIDAY

Standing on one foot
12 seconds/leg

Trunk twists on floor
20 seconds

One-legged toe touches
- 5/leg

Back leg raises
6/leg

Side leg raises
6/leg

Body circles (standing)
8/direction

Toe reaches (sitting on floor)
30 seconds/leg

Wall pushes
20 seconds/leg

Repeat 1 times for 2 total sets

Printed in Great Britain
by Amazon

19151927R00041